A TASTE OF MAMA NATURE

A Handbook For Vegans And Vegetarians
With Natural Recipes And Exercise Plans

PUBLISHED BY :
RESEARCH ASSOCIATES
SCHOOL TIMES PUBLICATIONS

A TASTE
of
MAMA NATURE

*A Handbook For Vegans And Vegetarians
With Natural Recipes And Exercise Plan
by*

ABOLADE NKOSI TAYO

FRONTLINE DISTRIBUTION INTERNATIONAL, INC.

751 EAST 75TH ST.	5937 WEST MADISON ST.
CHICAGO, IL 60619	CHICAGO, IL 60644
TEL#(312) 651-9888	TEL#(312) 626-1203
FAX#(312) 651-9850	FAX#(312) 626-1553

A TASTE
of
MAMA NATURE

First Published 1996
by
Research Associates   School Times Publications

and

FRONTLINE DISTRIBUTION INTERNATIONAL, INC.
© **1996 Abolade Nkosi Tayo**
Cover Design by Ammar

Library of Congress Card Catalog Number : 92-61499
ISBN : 0 94839 007 7

Published by
Research Associates
School Times Publications
751 East 75th Street
Chicago, IL 60619 U.S.A.

P.O. Box 4832
Arima, Trinidad, Caribbean
and
at Karnak House
300 Westbourne Park Road
London, WII, IEH,England •

CHICAGO • PHILADELPHIA • LONDON •
TRINIDAD, CARIBBEAN

A TASTE OF
MAMA NATURE

ayodele n'zingha tayo
30 years old
physical fitness enthusiast
and instructor.

4th degree black belt / aşa kiniun
(simba-ryu) afrikan martial arts
chief instructor - trinidad & tobago

CONTENTS PAGE

AUTHOR'S NOTE

The information given in this book is not meant to replace any physician or doctor's recommendation, it is not meant to substitute any professional medical advise, nor is it meant to be used as a cure to contradict your doctor or physician's advice.

The information, although researched, is the opinion of the author.

The exercise routines given must only be used after consulting your doctor or physician for his/her opinion showing him/her the information on the exercises given and getting his/her approval to begin exercising.

FOREWORD BY ABOLADE TAYO

You might ask the question, why another book on nutrition, when there are literally hundreds of good, well-researched books on nutrition which are also well written?

The answer is threefold:

1. There are relatively few books on veganism (total vegetarianism), as most vegetarian nutrition books include dairy products and some make use of eggs.

2. Most books on nutrition do not go into the other part of keeping healthy- exercise. This book not only recommends exercises, it tells you what type of exercise to do, what exercise program is best suited to you, etc.

3. This book shows you how to make nutritious meals and therefore it fills a gap. This book will appeal to the layman, to the keep-fit enthusiasts, the body builders, martial art practitioners and other sports persons.

I hope that reading this book will increase your knowledge on vegan nutrition. Research has revealed the hidden dangers in animal meat and products consumption. I hope you enjoy reading it.

CHAPTER 1

WHAT IS GOOD HEALTH?

Good health is the state of being free from pain and sickness; a vibrant good-to-be-alive feeling in mind, spirit and body.

Do you ever wake up feeling sleepy, tired, worn-out and just wanting to go back to bed? These are sure signs that all is not well with the body and it's time you did something about it.

To be healthy, you need vitamins, minerals, etc. In fact, you need a nutritious daily diet along with proper rest and exercise. Then you will truly know what it is to be healthy in body and mind, as in the famous saying: "A sound mind in a sound body."

Karatekas, body-builders, physical fitness enthusiasts and athletes should take more interest in their health, as they burn plenty of energy during training. This must be replaced by eating good food.

CHAPTER 2

PROPER NUTRITION

Proper nutrition is not something you leave to chance. It involves careful planning of what you eat or drink.

I make it a habit never to eat or drink anything questionable. As a rule I only eat fruits when I am away from home. If I visit a total vegetarian (vegan) home I may partake of food there, as vegans are more conscious, particular and more informed of what they eat or drink.

Proper nutrition means leaving out the garbage or junk food so easily available all around you, on the street corners, at the cafes, at the snackettes and even at the supermarkets.

Proper nutrition means using a properly planned diet which supplies all the nutrients necessary to your well-being, good health and strength.

This book was prepared for those who are seeking that goal.

CHAPTER 3

VITAMINS

Vitamins are necessary as they aid in digestion, the assimilation of foods, metabolism, etc.

Vitamins differ, but they are all of great importance to the body and to our existence.

Vitamins are found in foods, but it is a good idea to supplement them with a good vitamin-mineral tablet or capsule, especially if you do hard work or compete or take part in strenuous sports, such as karate, body-building, running etc.

You must be your own guide. You should know when you feel better and how many vitamin supplements to use.

Remember, it is the food you eat which determines the way you feel, so you should supplement your diet with food supplements and not the other way around.

Vitamin A

Vitamin A is one of the fat-soluble vitamins, meaning it dissolves in fat. This vitamin can be stored in the body.

It is necessary for good resistance to infection. It helps growth, promotes vigor, and protects against nutritional night blindness. It gives you protection against infection of the mucous membranes, eyes, nose, mouth, throat, bones, skin and soft tissues. It aids in making fast muscle gains.

Deficiency symptoms include infection of the mucous membranes, eyes, nose, mouth, throat, bones, skin, soft tissues, low resistance to infection, retarded growth, loss of vigor, poor vision, etc.

Good sources of vitamin A are butter, carrots, celery, cheese, lettuce, parsley, peaches, peas, prunes, soy beans, spinach, string beans, sunflower seeds, sweet potatoes, tomatoes, watercress and yellow corn.

Please note: When butter, cheese and milk are mentioned I am referring to Soya products.

Suggested Daily Ration (SDR) 25,000 I.U. Therapeutic Dose (TD) up to 50,000 I.U.

The Therapeutic doses are very good for body-builders and karatekas in hard training and people suffering from any deficiency symptoms mentioned.

Vitamin B

All the vitamins in this complex contain elements necessary for the nerves, energy and general well-being.

These belong to a different group from Vitamin A as they are water soluble, meaning that they dissolve in water, and you need them everyday, as the body cannot store them.

Vitamin B1 (Thiamine)

It is necessary for good appetite, weight-gain, good assimilation of food, resistance to fatigue, irritability, digestive upsets, neuritis, depression, insomnia, nervousness and dizziness. It is necessary for good muscle tone, growth and good circulation.

It protects against vague aches, pains, diarrhea and heart disorders, gas, low-thyroid activity, shortness of breath.

A very good source is brewer's yeast. Other good sources are blackstrap molasses, lentils, dry beans, nuts, peanuts, peas, wheat germ, soy beans, sunflower seeds.

Vitamin B2 (Riboflavin)

It is necessary for sound nerves, growth, good vision, healthy hair and skin. It protects you from dry hair, and skin, reddening lips, inflammation of the mouth, soreness of the tongue and poor vision.

A good source of this vitamin is brewer's yeast. Other good sources are wheat germ, green leafy vegetables, mangoes, prunes and soy beans.

Vitamin B5 (Nicotinamide)

It is necessary for healthy skin, nerves and intestines. It aids in preventing headaches and insomnia.

Good sources of this vitamin are brewer's yeast and wheat germ.

Vitamin B6 (Pyridoxine)

This is necessary for healthy skin and nerves. It gives energy and aids in conserving protein. A deficiency causes muscular disturbances, fatigue,

insomnia, irritability, heart troubles and intestinal disorders.

It strengthens the muscles, and plays an important part in utilizing fats and forming blood.

Good sources are brewer's yeast, blackstrap molasses, cabbage, corn, oil, nuts, seeds, cauliflower, onions, rice, watermelon, wheat germ, milk, peanut oil, banana, apple, raw carrot, soy beans, grapefruit juice and orange juice.

Vitamin B12 (Cyano- Cobalamin)

This is necessary for gaining weight, growth and healthy blood.

A deficiency can cause anemia, retarded growth, tiredness, paleness of skin, poor blood conditions, poor appetite, breathing difficulties, degeneration of cells in the central nervous system, migraine headaches, and sore tongue.

Good sources of this vitamin are brewer's yeast, wheat germ, tomatoes, corn and wheat.

Vitamin B-Complex (Biotin)

Deficiency causes lassitude, sleeplessness, dry skin and nervousness.

A good source of it is brewer's yeast, cauliflower, carrots, peanuts, spinach, onions, grapefruit, corn and wheat.

Vitamin B-Complex (Inositol)

It is necessary for normal intestinal activity, metabolism of fats and prevents premature aging.

Good sources are brewer's yeast, wheat germ, fruits and corn.

Vitamin B-Complex (Folic Acid)

It is necessary in dealing with some types of anemia. It regulates the activity of the liver and also aids in making red blood cells.

Good sources of this vitamin are brewer's yeast and wheat germ.

Vitamin B-Complex (Para-Amino-Benzoic Acid)

Aids in preventing anemia, skin disorders, fatigue, arthritis and delays the graying of the hair.

Good sources are brewer's yeast, blackstrap molasses, nuts, fruits, whole-wheat bread, cauliflower, soy beans, potatoes (sweet and white), oranges, peas and oats.

Vitamin B-Complex (Choline)

It controls the food fat distribution in the body, prevents premature aging, retards the hardening of arteries and minimizes the possibility of a heart attack.

Good sources of this vitamin are brewer's yeast, wheat germ, whole grains, peas, cabbage, fruits and soy beans.

Vitamin B-Complex (Pantothentic Acid)

Deficiency symptoms include skin disorders, adrenal upsets, burning feet etc.

It is important for the body's resistance to stress.

It metabolizes carbohydrates and assists in maintaining normal hormone balance.

Good sources of pantothenic acid are pecans, peanuts, wheat germ, brown rice and yeast.

Vitamin C

This Vitamin is water soluble and cannot be manufactured by the body. The body needs generous amounts of it daily. A dosage of 1,000 mg. daily is desirable to fight infection and maintain good health.

Deficiency symptoms include tooth decay, scurvy, gum infection, bleeding of the nose, mouth and face, muscular weakness, anemia, loss of appetite, pains in joints and restlessness.

Good sources of this important vitamin are rose hips, apples, avocados, bananas, cabbage, citrus fruits, peaches, green peppers, sweet corn, berries and cantaloupe (melon).

Vitamin D

This vitamin is fat soluble and is necessary for good health as it prevents rickets, tooth decay, bone deformities, muscular weakness, glandular conditions, and calcium and phosphorous deficiencies.

It is necessary for general health and helps in combating arthritis.

Good sources of this vitamin are sunflower seeds, beet, greens, cabbage, carrot tops and corn oil.

Vitamin E

This is necessary for preventing sterility, tiredness, premature aging, muscular and nervous disorders.

It has been used to relieve asthma, cataracts, diabetes, headaches,

muscular dystrophy and many other complaints.

It is especially necessary for body-builders, athletes in hard training, as it is very good for the heart.

Good sources are wheat germ, apples, avocados, bananas, carrots, corn oil, kelp, lettuce, peanut oil, peas, soy bean oil, sweet potatoes, tomatoes.

Vitamin F

This is necessary in building good health, healthy skin, sound nerves and growth.

Good sources are wheat germ oil, corn oil, sunflower oil, soy bean oil, peanut oil and peanuts.

Vitamin K

This is what causes the blood to clot, so it is necessary especially in cases of injuries, tooth extraction, childbirth and surgery.

It is particularly found in cabbage, tomatoes, soy beans, wheat, corn, wheat germ, cauliflower, peas and leafy greens.

Vitamin P

This is necessary for the health of the heart and blood vessel walls. It slows down degeneration of the body. It is necessary in preventing high blood pressure, miscarriage and diabetes.

Good sources of this vitamin are citrus fruits, grapes, prunes, rose hips, spinach, green peppers, black and red currants and parsley.

CHAPTER 4
MINERALS

These are all important to good health as each plays an important role in the upkeep of your body.

They are necessary in reconditioning and preserving blood, bones, brains, hair, heart, muscles, nerves and teeth - in fact, all the functions of the body.

Good sources are almonds, blackstrap molasses, nuts, cheese, milk, potatoes and soy beans.

Chlorine

Deficiency can cause slow growth, anxiety and uneasiness. It is necessary as a blood-cleanser.

Good sources are beets, radishes and leafy greens.

Copper

This is necessary for healthy sex glands and the prevention of anemia. It aids bone marrow in the production of red blood cells in conjunction with iron and iodine.

Good sources are almonds, prunes, soy flour, blackstrap molasses and green vegetables.

Iodine

This is vital: lack of iodine can result in death. Most of it can be found in the thyroid gland and it is necessary for its proper functioning.

It relieves nervous tension and gives great endurance and stamina. It promotes growth and is very important for good health.

Deficiency of this mineral may cause over-weight, lowered mentality and goiter.

Good sources are garlic, bananas, carrots, celery, fruits, lettuce, peanuts, peas, tomatoes and seeds.

Iron

A deficiency of this mineral can cause anemia, premature graying, wrinkling of the skin, brittle fingernails, poor heartbeat, unhealthy skin, shortness of breath and inflamed mouth and tongue.

Good sources are wheat germ, whole grains, raisins, prunes, peanuts, blackstrap molasses, brewer's yeast and apricots.

Magnesium

Without this your body would be unhealthy. Your muscles would not function at their best, and your bone structure would be poor.

Good sources are wheat germ, blackstrap molasses, cashew nuts, peanuts, sunflower seeds, pumpkin seeds, kelp and dried lima beans.

Phosphorous

This is necessary for muscle contraction. It builds strong bones and teeth, aids in growth, and is necessary for good appetite, strength, and weight gain. It assists in the digestion of carbohydrates and fats.

Good sources are cheese, whole grains, soy beans and beet tops.

Potassium

This is necessary for healthy nerves and heart, normal growth, energy and resistance to colds. A deficiency may cause indigestion and muscle spasms, proneness to colds and can lead to heart failure.

Good sources are almonds, apple juice, carrots, blackstrap molasses, apple cider vinegar, prunes, fruits, watercress, potatoes and tomatoes.

Silicon

This is necessary for good skin, strong bones, sound teeth, healthy hair, resistance to infection and firm skin.

Good sources are brewer's yeast, apple cider vinegar, fruits and sunflower seeds.

Sulphur

This is necessary for strengthening the bloodstream, and for promoting good hair and nail health. It helps the liver to assimilate minerals, and promotes bile secretion.

Good sources are garlic, cabbage, carrots, peaches and radishes.

Zinc

This is necessary for general body health and is present in all tissues.

Good sources are oranges, barley, oatmeal, cabbage, whole wheat bread, carrots, lettuce, peas, peanut butter and rice.

A number of other minerals are also necessary for good health: boron, bromine, cobalt, fluorine, silver, nickel and manganese.

Good sources are beets, lentils, nuts, tomatoes, peas, carrots and green beans.

CHAPTER 5

FATS

Fat is necessary for your very existence. Without it life would be impossible.

One of its main functions is to provide a large reserve of readily available energy. It also serves as a vehicle for the absorption of essential fat-soluble vitamins. It is composed of fatty acids and steroids.

Fat is a major source of heat and energy, which is necessary for the body's healthy operation.

Fat also provides an energy reserve when stored in the body in reasonable amounts. It protects the vital organs and insulates against high temperature.

Good sources are rice, wheat germ, avocado, cashews, coconut, vegetable margarine, peanuts, peanut butter, peanut oil, vegetable shortening, soy beans, corn oil, sesame seeds, pigeon peas, watermelon seeds, cornmeal, almonds, pecans, safflower oil and palm oil.

CHAPTER 6
CARBOHYDRATES

Carbohydrates are necessary to assist in the digestion and assimilation of other foods, they are the chief source of energy for all body functions.

Calories from carbohydrates are immediately available for energy by producing heat in the body when carbon in the system unites with oxygen in the blood stream.

They also help regulate protein and fat metabolism. Fats require carbohydrates for their breakdown within the liver.

Carbohydrates can be manufactured in the body from some amino acids and the glycerol compounds of fats.

Some are definitely to be avoided as they contribute to ill-health. Carbohydrates like this are found in soft drinks, white bread, pastries, white sugar and their products.

There are some that are definitely of value to your body. They contribute to your health as they contain vitamins, minerals and enzymes.

Combined with fats, they keep up and invigorate the body and supply vitality and warmth.

Carbohydrates cannot and must not be substituted for protein. Whatever your source, make sure the combination is made up of proteins, vitamins and minerals, fats and carbohydrates.

Good sources of wholesome carbohydrates are potatoes, blackstrap molasses, red kidney beans, green lima beans, cabbage, corn, carrots, beet root, cucumbers, parsley, peppers, okras, onions, lentils, eggplant (melongene), soy beans, apples, cantaloupes, apple cider vinegar, avocados, tomatoes, tomato ketchup (catsup), nectar and bananas.

CHAPTER 7

PROTEINS

Protein is essential for a healthy body: a body existing on a poor protein diet cannot be fit or healthy.

Proteins are the body's building blocks and are absolutely necessary for your existence.

They are so important that you cannot really exist without them. They are needed for constructing new body tissues during the growth, maintenance, renewal and repair of the body right through life.

Blood hemoglobin is 95 per cent protein. Tissues, organs, skin, hair, nails, bones, nerves and the fluids secreted by the body are made of protein.

Amino acids construct proteins. Ten of them are absolutely indispensable as they cannot be made by the body.

Essential Amino Acids

Phenylalanine, Methionine, Leucine, Valine, Lysine, Isoleucine, Threo-nine, Tryptophan, Histidine & Arginine.

Histidine is essential for children, but not for adults. Children do not need Arginine.

Non-essential Amino Acids

Glycine, Alanine, Proline, Serine, Cystine, Norleucine, Trysonine, Glutamic Acid, Citrulline, Aspartic Acid, Hydroxy-proline and Hydroxyglutamic acid.

Foods that contain all ten of them are called complete protein foods. These are peanuts and soy beans.

Other good protein foods are dried beans, whole grain cereals, dried peas and lentil, although these do not contain all the amino acids.

Although 'incomplete protein foods' should be used only in conjunction with complete proteins, they play an important role and can be obtained at a lower cost.

Protein deficiency causes low resistance to infection, and slow healing of wounds. The liver is more prone to injury, the body becomes waterlogged, anemia results, growth ceases, high blood pressure steps in and you never enjoy real good health.

A high protein supplement is very important as it is cheap and is a very

good source of complete protein. Soya milk powder is highly recommended as such.

CHAPTER 8

HEALTH FOODS

There are natural health foods that are necessary for health and strength. They are particularly important for body-builders, athletes, keep-fit enthusiasts, karatekas, and for anyone interested in strength, health and well-built physiques.

Blackstrap Molasses

This is very good as it contains B vitamins and aids in combating fatigue, constipation and many other common complaints. A tablespoon a day is a very good rule to follow.

Brewer's Yeast

This is very good as it is a nutritious source of protein, B vitamins and minerals. It is so valuable that persons who use it feel good, and those who start using it feel the benefit of it in a short time. You can use it in powder, flakes or tablet form.

Apple Cider Vinegar

This is exceptionally good as it aids in quieting migraine headaches and has been proven to fight harmful bacteria.

It rebuilds the body and helps to combat colds and influenza, bronchitis, etc.

It helps blood circulation, and it normalizes and improves metabolism and digestion.

It is highly recommended to sufferers of chronic headaches, high blood pressure, sore throat, nose bleeding, arthritis, etc.

It contains fluorine, iron, phosphorous, magnesium, silicon, sodium, sulfur, calcium, chlorine and other trace minerals.

Put two teaspoons of apple cider vinegar in a glass of water and sip it slowly. Try this daily and see how your health improves.

Garlic

This contains many nutrients essential for good health. It is an internal disinfectant and combats colds, bronchitis and many other complaints. Use

four garlic pearls daily and feel better. (You can chew garlic, if you desire: about two grains daily.)

Sunflower Seeds

These are good sources of proteins, vitamins and minerals which are beneficial to the whole body.

You would do well to use a concentrate of this wonder food daily.

Wheat Germ

This wonder food contains many vitamins, minerals and other necessary nutrients. It is especially noted as a valuable source of vitamin E, the wonder vitamin.

It is important as a heart food and can be used generally, as it comes in various forms; flakes, capsules and tablets. Make sure you use it in one form or another daily.

Soy Bean

Contrary to what some nutritionists teach, mankind can live healthy, strong and well nourished, without consuming any animal product whatsoever.

The soy bean is man's key to sound health as milk, cheese, butter etc., are made from it. Nutritionally, it has no equal. Here are reliable documented facts about it.

It contains twice as much protein as beef. The protein found in it is of high quality with all the essential amino acids in high proportions.

It contains more iron than beef. It contains more than ten (10) times the amount of protein as cow's milk.

It has over twenty times more vitamin B than beef. It contains more protein than eggs.

Soy milk is more easily digested than cow's.

It can be used in supplementing the diets of athletes who must use extra protein such as body-builders, weight-lifters, power-lifters, karatekas (Awon Akeko Lati Si), runners etc.

It also contains generous quantities of vitamin E, B-complex, vitamin F, K and minerals.

What to do

Now you know of some of nature's wonder foods, try to add some to your diet. You will build a healthy, strong body.

CHAPTER 9

HEALTH FOOD SUPPLEMENTS

Some people, including doctors and nutritionists, contend that if sufficient nutritious foods are eaten or taken in liquid form, health food supplements are not necessary.

I agree with that, if 'sufficient' means all that the body needs daily to be in good health.

However, I have handled many cases involving people who had been written off by medical science as hopeless and they have all responded well to vitamin and mineral treatment.

Even everyday cases of tiredness, frequent colds, pains in the body etc., can be traced to a lack of certain vitamins, minerals or protein.

I have personally used (and still do) vitamin and mineral supplements plus added quantities of vitamins C, E and B with great results.

As a vegetarian, however, I have been able to feel better using fewer supplements- compared to those I used when I ate eggs, cheese, cow's milk, meat, fish, etc.

In fact my body's system (in general) has improved because of my vegetarian (vegan) diet.

I suggest that you read this book and you will see in which area you need to use more vitamins, minerals, etc. In the meantime, use a good vitamin/mineral tablet. I say tablet and not capsule because sometimes the capsule itself is made from an animal source (animal gelatin).

However if you use animal products my advice is to cut down on the amount used (see Chapter 22 on vegetarianism for a more detailed analysis).

CHAPTER 10

EXERCISE AND REST

Exercise is essential and vital to the body's health and proper functioning. Muscles which are not too active get soft and flabby, and other organs grow weak. The body was built for activity.

Not everybody will want to do strenuous exercises, but then, even walking is good exercise for someone who drives around or is driven most of the time.

Exercise tones and strengthens the muscles and internal organs. Exercise clears the mind, especially when you are in the type of work where you use your brains far more than your muscles.

It builds a sound body which combined with a sound mind is very good. Regular, constructive exercise encourages you to eat properly, to watch your diet closely, to be more concerned with what you put into your mouth.

If you consume garbage or junk foods you will not enjoy the type of well-being that is possible with a good diet.

There are various types of exercises, from walking and running to heavy weight training, aerobics, lightweight training, moderate weight training and serious body-building. Sports that are good forms of exercise include road walking, running, cycling, football, karate and the martial arts.

For more details on exercise and exercising, read Chapters 12-18

Next we must consider rest, as no lasting benefits can come from exercising if you are not getting sufficient rest. The amount of rest any person should take depends on the individual involved, I usually recommend 7 to 9 hours of sleep, but it does depend on the individual.

If you sleep 6 hours each night and awake feeling fit, full of energy and ready to go, and you maintain this high for most of the day, then 6 hours are enough for you. The same goes for the individual who gets 7,8,9 or more hours of sleep.

I should point out that children actively engaged in sports need 8 to 10 hours of sleep each night.

The importance of rest cannot be over-emphasized. The body rebuilds itself as you sleep.

CHAPTER 11

WHAT IS A GOOD DIET?

This is a big question, with a simple answer. A good diet is one that contains all the nutrients the body needs for well-being, and for optimum health.

A good diet must consist of fruits, fruit juices, vegetables, soya products, peas, beans, ground provisions, rice, herbs (parsley, thyme, etc.), garlic, onions, etc. A good diet will make you feel good all day. For more details on a good diet read Chapters 9 and 23.

If you want to eat good wholesome foods and consume nutritious drinks, you must know your nutrients (vitamin, minerals, proteins, fats, carbohydrates). Ignorance of these could determine how long you take to start consuming a good diet.

A good diet calls for the proper combinations of food and drink.

Most people eat, then flush down the food with a big drink. This can cause gas to form in your body.

I never recommend eating then drinking, but if you must drink, never use an acid drink (orange, grapefruit, passion fruit, juices, etc.) after consuming starchy foods such as rice, potatoes, dasheen, yams, yucca (cassava), macaroni, spaghetti, etc. Instead sip a glass of mauby, banana punch, paw paw punch, soya milk, etc. The best advice is to drink no less than 45 minutes to one hour after eating, and even so the latter drinks are recommended.

Your meals should be colorful and attractive, and you should eat salads as often as possible with your meals.

You should spend some time reading vegetarian and Vegan (total vegetarian) literature.

You should personally mix some of your drinks and cook some of your food, or at least assist in preparing them, as this will increase your knowledge in this field.

Sodas should be avoided, although they are better than nothing. Fruit drinks or fruits cost no more than a soda and are better for you. You must think good living and live good.

CHAPTER 12

PHYSICAL FITNESS WITHOUT WEIGHTS

Many persons when hearing the words physical fitness or exercise immediately think of weight-training, which is wrong. Although I personally feel that weight training is the best and most economical way of keeping fit, whether it be light, moderate or heavy weight training, you can be physically fit without ever touching a bar bell or machines using weights. Here, however, I will deal with physical fitness without weights.

There are numerous forms of free-style exercising without weights, such as walking. Anyone taking up walking as exercise should begin gradually, especially if that person was not very active physically. First just walk a few yards, taking your time, then you can gradually increase the distance, making it half a block, then a whole block. Then you can start walking briskly, making a block or two or more. Next we come to jogging. Jogging should not be done suddenly, like walking, start with a brisk walk, a moderate jog, a brisk walk, then a moderate jog, etc.

Next we come to calisthenics. You need a broomstick, two books and a bench (the bench is not absolutely necessary).

Here is the routine:
1. Heel raises with broomstick
2. Squats with broomstick on back
3. Straight armed pullovers on floor or bench
4. Side laterals with books, lying on bench
5. Standing forward raises with broomstick
6. Standing side laterals with books
7. Bent forward rowing to waist with broomstick
8. Triceps dips
9. Sit ups
10. Knee pushouts

First you warm up by doing brisk running on the spot, then you proceed to do one set of heel raises 15 times (illustration 1). Rest 2 minutes, then move on to exercise 2 (illustration 2 & 3), squats with broomstick on back. Place a broomstick on your back as shown in illustration. 2, keep your back straight,

bending your legs you squat down to position shown in illustration. 3, breathe in as you go down, then return to position shown in illustration. 2, breathing out all the way as you come up. This constitutes one repetition (afterwards referred to as rep, plural reps). Perform 4 more reps, then move on to <u>exercise 3</u>, which is called straight armed pullovers on the floor or on a bench. Lie on the floor as shown in illustration 4, then bring your arms up in a semicircular movement to position shown in illustration. 5. Perform this, exercise 5 reps, resting 2 minutes before going on to the next exercise.

<u>Exercise 4</u>, illustration 6, you start with both hands touching above the body, then move both arms outward to position shown, breathing in, as you do so, then return both arms to starting position, breathing out as you do so.

<u>Exercise 5</u> stand as shown in illustration 7, then slowly raise the stick forward and up, breathing in until it reaches overhead as shown in illustration 8, breathing out as you return to starting position. Repeat this exercise 15 times then rest 2 minutes before moving on to the next exercise.

<u>Exercise 6</u> stand as shown in illustration 9, slowly raising your hands to the side and upwards breathing in as you do so, until they reach the position shown in illustration 10, then slowly lower your hands, breathing out until you return to starting position. Repeat 15 times then rest 2 minutes before starting the next exercise.

<u>Exercise 7</u>, bend forward as shown in illustration 11, then slowly raise the broomstick until it touches your waist, as shown in illustration 12, breathing in as you do so, then breathing out as you slowly lower the broomstick to starting position, repeating 15 times. Rest 2 minutes before starting the next exercise.

<u>Exercise 8</u>, assume the position shown in illustration 13, then as you return slowly to the position shown in illustration 2 breathe out. Repeat 5 times, then rest 2 minutes before starting next exercise.

<u>Exercise 9</u>, assume position shown in illustration 15, then as you come up to position shown in illustration 16, breathe in, then breathe out as you slowly return to starting position. Repeat 15 times, then rest 2 minutes before starting the next exercise.

<u>Exercise 10</u>, assume position shown in illustration 17, breathing in as you slowly push your knees and feet out to position shown in illustration 18, then breathing out as you slowly return your knees and feet to starting position. Repeat 15 times, then rest.

You can train on alternate days, for example Sunday-Tuesday-Thursday-

Saturday-Monday-Wednesday etc.). This means you would train four days per week sometimes and three days sometimes.

Before you begin exercising, you should warm up by doing running on the spot, briskly moving your legs and arms as you do so. Then you proceed to exercise through exercise 3. This constitutes your workout for day one. On day two, you add exercise 4, on day three, you add exercise 5, on day four, you add exercise 6, on day five you add exercise 7, on day six you add exercise 8, on day seven, you add exercise 9, on day eight, you add exercise 10, on day nine you perform each exercise 3 sets of 15 reps resting 2 minutes between sets before going on to the next exercise.

You can use this routine for three to four months, before going on to another routine, or until you get your desired results.

Never exercise on a full stomach. Allow 1 1/2 hours or more after eating solid foods before you exercise or one hour after drinking a large glass or two of liquid food.

PHYSICAL FITNESS WITHOUT WEIGHTS

exercise 1
illustration1
heel raises with
or without broomstick

exercise 2
illustration 2
squats with broom stick
starting position

PHYSICAL FITNESS WITHOUT WEIGHTS

illustration 3
squats with broom stick

exercise 3 illustration 4
straight armed
pullovers on floor or bench starting position

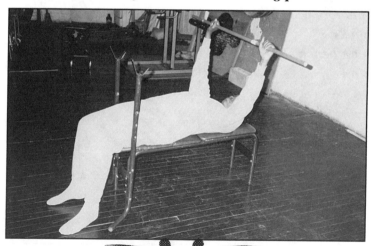

PHYSICAL FITNESS WITHOUT WEIGHTS

exercise 3
illustration 5
straight armed pullover
floor or bench

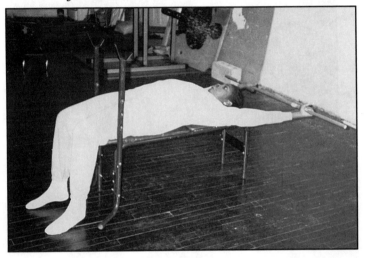

exercise 4
illustration 6
side laterals with barbells
or, books
lying on bench - starting
position

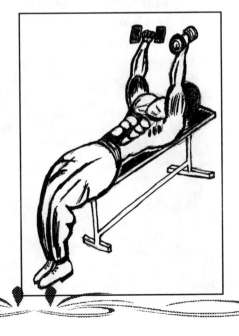

PHYSICAL FITNESS WITHOUT WEIGHTS

exercise 4
illustration 7
side laterals with light dumbbells or,
books

exercise 5
illustration 8
standing forward raises
with broomstick -
starting position

PHYSICAL FITNESS WITHOUT WEIGHTS

exercise 5
illustration 9
standing forward raises
with broomstick

PHYSICAL FITNESS WITHOUT WEIGHTS

exercise 6
illustration 10
standing laterals with
books - standing position

exercise 6
illustration 11
 standing side laterals
with books

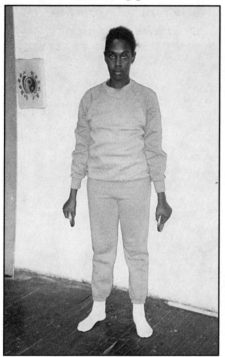

PHYSICAL FITNESS WITHOUT WEIGHTS

exercise 7
illustration 12
bent forward rowing to waist
with broomstick
starting position

exercise 7
illustration 13
bent forward rowing to
waist with broomstick

PHYSICAL FITNESS WITHOUT WEIGHTS

exercise 7
photo 14
triceps dips starting position

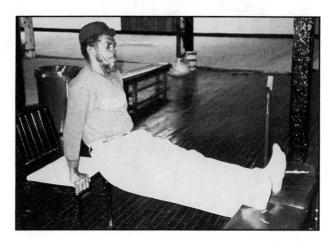

exercise 7
photo 15
triceps dips

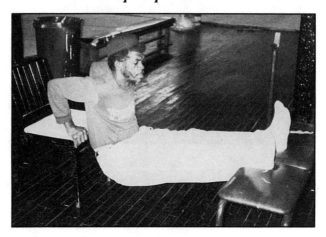

PHYSICAL FITNESS WITHOUT WEIGHTS

ʟexercise 9
illustration 16
situps - starting position

exercise 9
illustration 17
situps

PHYSICAL FITNESS WITHOUT WEIGHTS

exercise 10
illustration 18
knee pushouts -
starting position

exercise 10
illustration 19
knee pushouts

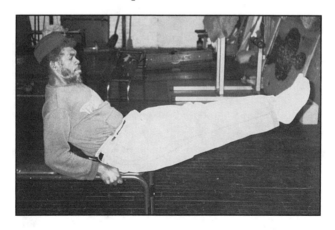

CHAPTER 13

MARTIAL ARTS

Martial arts as exercise can be very rewarding. You will not only be fit, but you will know how to defend yourself effectively.

The best form of martial arts for keeping fit is weaponry using the long staff, sword, etc. I personally recommend the long staff accompanied by kicking.

There are many forms of martial arts. Empty hand kata or weaponry kata are good ways to keep fit. Last but not least (as this builds a great deal of fitness) is karate training.

Whatever style of karate or martial arts you choose you can use, I personally recommend Simba-Ryu (Asa Kiniun) Afrikan martial arts. I am the Chief Instructor, and have been practising martial arts for over 35 years.

As I said at the beginning of this chapter, martial arts done properly can build a fit, healthy physique. Many of my students have built really well developed physiques with martial arts, and I rate it for keeping fit.

Here are a few karate movements, which can be used to keep you fit:
1. Warm-up exercise - running on the spot
2. Floor dips
3. Alternate punching
4. Alternate jabbing
5. Thrusting front kick to the chest
6. Thrusting side kick to the chest
7. Cutting kick to the knee
8. Roundhouse kick to the chest
9. Sit-ups
10. Knee push-outs

You can start off with 1 set of 10 reps in each exercise on three alternate days each week (Mon-Wed-Fri or Tues-Thurs-Sat etc.). On the second week move on to 2 sets, 3rd week 3 sets, 4th week 4 sets, 5th week 5 sets. Sit-ups and knee push-outs reps can be increased to 25 to 50 Reps.

These exercises are for persons who have knowledge of karate or other martial arts. Beginners with no martial arts training are not advised to use this routine.

MARTIAL ARTS TRAINING

illustration 1a   *illustration 1b*
running on the spot   *running on the spot*

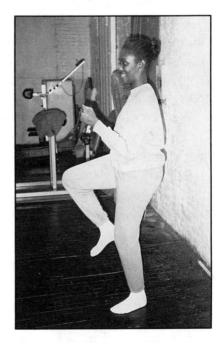

illustration 2a
floor dips

MARTIAL ARTS TRAINING

illustration 2b
floor dips

illustration 3
alternate punching

illustration 4
alternate jabbing

MARTIAL ARTS TRAINING

5. rising front kick   *6.. thrusting side kick to chest*

MARTIAL ARTS TRAINING

7. cutting kick to the knee

*8. round house kick
to the chest*

MARTIAL ARTS TRAINING

9. sit-ups

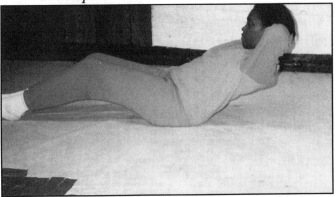

10-A knee pushouts

10-B knee pushouts

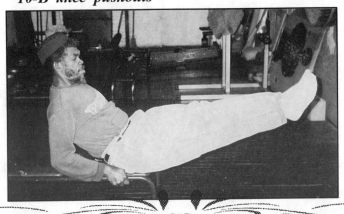

CHAPTER 14

WEIGHT-TRAINING

As I said before, in my opinion weight-training is the most economical way to keep fit.

If you are interested in keeping fit with weight-training, you can either join a gym or health studio, or purchase a set of weights with instructions and train at home or you can read the instructions given at the end of this chapter, carefully performing the exercises given.

But, before embarking on any exercise program you should consult your doctor, have a general check-up and ask your doctor for his opinion

Here is a routine which I recommend for keeping fit and toning the muscles:

1. Heel raises	3 sets of 20 reps
2. Parallel squats	3 sets of 12 reps
3. Straight arm pullovers - Lying on the floor	3 sets of 12 reps
4. Lying barbell bench presses	3 sets of 12 reps
5. Standing barbell presses	3 sets of 12 reps
6. Barbell curls standing - medium grip	3 sets of 12 reps
7. Seated barbell wrist curls	3 sets of 12 reps
8. Sit-ups	3 sets of 20 reps
9. Knee push-outs	3 sets of 20 reps

First, I will give you a step by step guide as to what to do. A rep (the short term for repetition) denotes the beginning and completion of an exercise. Reps are 2 or more consecutive complete movements of the said exercise, and the completion of multiple reps constitutes one set of the exercise performed.

You can train on 3 alternate days, Monday-Wednesday and Friday or Sunday-Tuesday and Thursday or Tuesday-Thursday and Saturday. You begin by performing a set of each exercise from 1 to 4, using the bar alone, no additional weights. On the second day you add 5 to 9, performing each exercise one set each.

On the second week use 2 sets of each exercise, and on the 3rd week 3 sets.

WEIGHT TRAINING

1. heel raises

2. parallel squats

WEIGHT TRAINING

3. straight arms
pullovers on flat bench

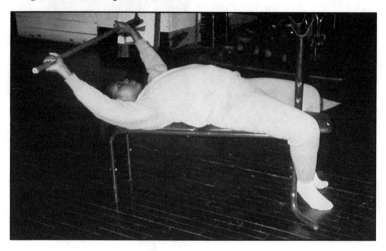

4. barbell flat bench presses

WEIGHT TRAINING

**5. standing
barbell presses**

*6. standing barbell
medium gripcurls*

WEIGHT TRAINING

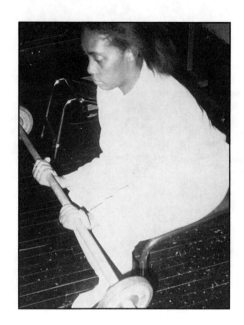

7. seated palms up wrist curls with barbells

8. sit-ups

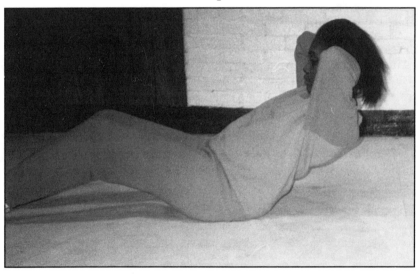

9. knee pushouts

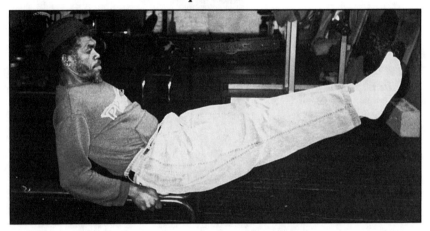

CHAPTER 15

BODY-BUILDING

Body-building with weights cannot fail to build a good physique if you follow common sense and don't go overboard.

A word of caution. If you want to build a championship physique, you do not have to take steroids (drugs) to speed up your weight gains. This might look <u>attractive now,</u> but it is certainly <u>destructive in the future</u>, as it defeats the original purpose, that of building <u>good health and keeping fit.</u>

I have seen many of my body-building students go from skinny bodies to really massive physiques.

The fastest way to gain weight naturally is to use a vegan (total vegetarian) diet. Read chapter 22 of this book on vegetarianism, which tells you how to make the changeover gradually and safely with lasting results. You must consult your doctor before embarking on a body building program with weights.

Here is a body-building program which I recommend. This is not for the beginner but for the more advanced body-builder, one who has been training for at least six months. Beginners should read Chapter 4, as the program outlined there is not only for keeping fit, but it's an excellent beginners routine.

More advanced (intermediate) body-builders, will be acquainted with the terms sets and reps. I have two routines, one to be done on a particular day, followed by the other on the day immediately following. Then you rest one day, then you repeat, then rest two days.

Here are some examples:

Sundays - routine A	Mondays - routine A
Mondays - routine B	Tuesdays - routine B
Tuesdays - rest	Wednesdays - rest
Wednesdays - routine A *OR*	Thursdays -routine A
Thursdays - routine B	Fridays - routine B
Fridays & Saturdays - rest	Saturdays & Sundays - rest

Or you can arrange your own days patterned along with the

examples I give you:

4th day - routine A
5th day - routine B
6th day - rest
7th day - rest

Here are the routines. Please follow all instructions precisely, as this will ensure success.

Routine A

Thighs: Chest: Deltoids: Abdominals:
Thighs
    1. Hack squats   5 sets 8-10 reps
    2. Parallel squats   5 sets 8-10 reps
Chest
    1. Multi bar bent arm pullovers on flat bench   5 sets 8-10 reps
    2. Inclined barbell bench presses (med. to wide grip) 5 sets 8-10 reps
    3. Inclined dumbbell laterals (flyes)   5 sets 8-10 reps
Deltoids
    1. Seated barbell presses behind neck   5 sets 8-10 reps
    2. Seated dumbbell presses   5 sets 8-10 reps
Abdominals
    1. Knee push-outs   5 sets 20 reps
    2. Twisting sit-ups   5 sets 20 reps

Routine B

Back: Arms: Forearms: Calves:
Back
    1. Wide chins behind neck or lat machine pull-ups   5 sets 8-10 reps
    2. Bent forward multi-bar rowing to waist   5 sets 8-10 reps
Arms
    1. Standing lat. machine (triceps) pull downs   5 sets 8-10 reps
    2. Seated multi-bar triceps curls   5 sets 8-10 reps
    3. Seated alternate dumbbell curls   5 sets 8-10 reps
Forearms
    1. Seated palms up swing bell wrist curls   5 sets 10-2 reps

    2. Seated palms down wrist curls   5 sets 10-2 reps

Calves

      1. Heel raises on calf machine - standing   5 sets 25 reps

      2. Heel raises on calf machine - seated   5 sets 25 reps

Start off with 1 set in each exercise on 1st and 2nd workout days, on 3rd and 4th days use 2 sets, on 2nd week 3 sets, 4th week 4 sets, 6th week 5 sets.

CHAPTER 16

REDUCING

Reducing can be done safely using calisthenics or weight-training.

Again, you should first consult your doctor for advice, then you can join any of the health studios which have good reputations and programs. In this way you would be guided step by step by a qualified instructor, who would demonstrate to you the proper way to perform the necessary exercises.

A vegetarian diet will be of great value to you, as you will be eating fewer calories, and more nutritious foods.

I also recommend the following routine which can be done at home, which combines calisthenics and weight-training. Please read carefully and follow the instructions, after consulting your doctor.

Mondays-Wednesdays and Fridays or Sundays-Tuesdays and

Thursdays

1. Half way sit-ups	5 sets-50 reps
2. Knee push-outs	5 sets-50 reps
3. Standing twists	5 sets-50 reps
4. Standing forward raises with bar	5 sets-25 reps
5. Straight arm pullovers on bench with bar	5 sets-25 reps
6. Dumbbell laterals(flyes) on inclined bench	5 sets-25 reps
7. Bent forward barbell row to waist	5 sets-25 reps
8. Seated barbell triceps curls	5 sets-25 reps
9. Standing barbell biceps curls	5 sets-25 reps
10. Seated palms up wrist curls	5 sets-25 reps
11. Leg extensions or parallel squats	5 sets-25 reps
12. Leg curls or hack squats	5 sets-25 reps
13. Heel raises on calf machine or barbell heel raises	5 sets-30 reps

Please consult your doctor before starting this program, and read carefully and make sure you understand the instructions before you begin.

You should begin this program gradually, and in fact you should not be using the entire program until the 7th week.

You begin by doing a set of 6 reps in exercise no. 1, 4, and 9. On the 2nd day of training you increase the reps to 8, on the 3rd day you add exercise 10, increasing the reps to 12. After this you add 2 reps to each exercise on each workout day until you are using the full number of reps recommended. Keep adding exercises each week until you are using the full routine, then add one

day of training you increase the reps to 8, on the 3rd day you add exercise 10, increasing the reps to 12. After this you add 2 reps to each exercise on each workout day until you are using the full number of reps recommended. Keep adding exercises each week until you are using the full routine, then add one set to each exercise each week, until you are using the full sets.

Note: You must always warm up, before beginning the routine, running on the spot, waving your arms as you do so.

1. halfway situps from floors

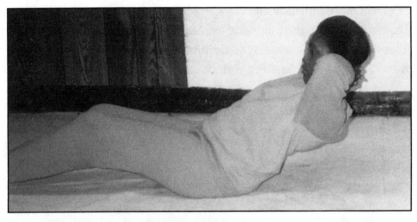

2. knee pushouts

REDUCING

*3. standing twists
with broomsticks
(or very light bar)*

*4. standing
forward raises with bar*

REDUCING

**5. straight arm pullovers
on bench with barbells**

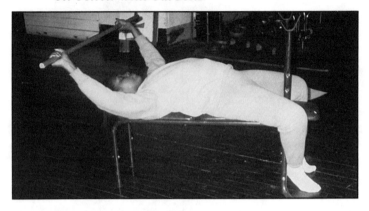

**6. dumbbell
laterals
on inclined bench**

REDUCING

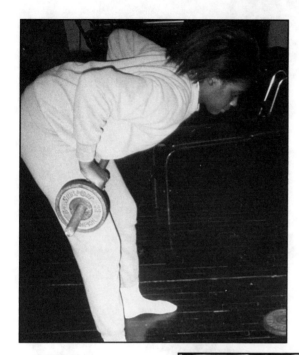

*7. bent forward
row to waist*

*8. seated barbell
triceps curls*

REDUCING

*9. standing
barbell biceps curls*

*10. seated palms up
barbells wrist curls*

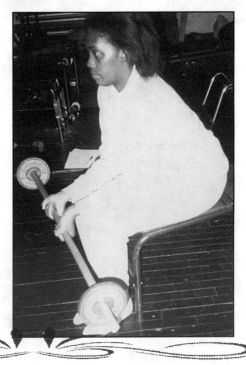

REDUCING

11. parallel squats

*12. hack squats
with barbells*

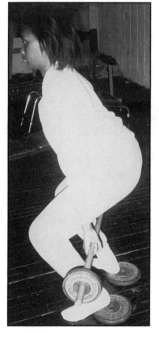

13. barbell heel raises
or heel raises on calf machine

CHAPTER 17

WEIGHT-GAINING

Gaining weight is a problem to millions of people worldwide. Some want to gain a few pounds and others more, some want a trim physique, others a more massive one. After consulting your doctor, you can use the following program, after carefully reading the instructions. In conjunction with a proper diet as explained in chapters 19 and 22 of this book, these exercises, along with proper rest and health food supplements, will add pounds of 'healthy muscles' to your body.

Here is the routine, with detailed instructions. You must train on three alternate days, Sunday, Tuesday and Thursday or Monday, Wednesday, and Friday.

1. Heel raises with barbell or calf machine   5 sets - 20 reps
2. Parallel squats   5 sets - 8 reps
3. Bent arm barbell pullovers on flat bench   5 sets - 8 reps
4. Barbell flat bench presses   5 sets - 8 reps
5. Standing barbell front presses   5 sets - 8 reps
6. Bent forward barbell rows to waist   5 sets - 8 reps
7. Standing barbell medium grip barbell biceps curls   5 sets - 8 reps
8. Sit-ups   5 sets- 15 to 20 reps

This program is simple but very effective in gaining weight. Follow the program given, after consulting your doctor. Train on 3 alternate days as recommended above.

On the first work-out day perform a set of reps of exercises I and 2, on the second work-out day use 2 sets of the same exercises, on the 3rd work-out day 3 sets, the 4th day 4 sets and the 5th day 5 sets. On the sixth day add exercises 3 and 4 performing 2 sets of reps, on the seventh day add exercise 5 performing 2 sets of reps, on day eight add exercise 6 performing 2 sets of reps, on the ninth day add exercise 7 performing 2 sets of reps, on the tenth day add exercise 8 performing 2 sets of reps, on the eleventh day add a set of reps to exercises 3 to 8 doing 4 sets of reps, on the twelfth day add a set of reps to exercises 3 to 8 doing 4 sets of reps, on the thirteenth day add a set of

WEIGHT GAINING
1.heel raises on calf machine

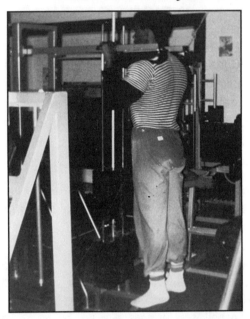

2. parallel squats

WEIGHT GAINING

3. bent arm
pullovers
on flat bench

4. barbell
bench presses

WEIGHT GAINING

5. *seated or standing barbell presses*

6. *bent forward barbell row to waist*

WEIGHT GAINING

7. standing barbell
medium grip barbell curls

8. sit-ups

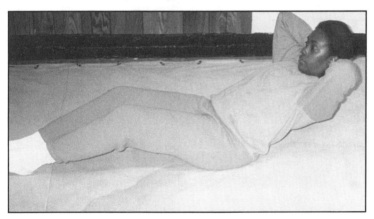

reps to exercises 3 to 8 doing 5 sets of reps. Now you are doing the full routine, you can use this routine for three to four months, then move on to the advanced routine given in Chapter 15.

Take your time, move gradually, start off with light poundages, then move on to moderate poundages, adding more as your strength increases. I recommend training with a partner so that you can help each other.

CHAPTER 18

SPOT SPECIALIZATION

To the ordinary person the term 'spot specialization' may simply be a problem of what to do about a bulging waist line, skinny legs or a sunken chest or skinny arms. To a body-builder, however, it would mean adding a few inches to already bulging arms, legs, calves or chest. However, this chapter is not for the body-builder, but for the ordinary person.

Most persons have a waistline problem, so I would confine this spot specialization to the abdominals. You can work out your abdominals up to 5 days weekly with good results, but please consult your doctor before embarking on this exercise program.

1. Sit-ups - halfway up	4 sets - 20 to 50 reps
2. Standing twists	4 sets - 20 to 50 reps
3. Twisting sit-ups	4 sets - 20 to 50 reps
4. Knee push-outs	4 sets - 20 to 50 reps
5. Bend over twists	4 sets - 20 to 50 reps

You begin by training 3 days on the first week, 4 days on the third week and 5 days on the fifth week.

Perform 1 set of 10 reps or less of exercise 1 on your first day, on the 2nd day, do exercise 2, performing a set of each exercise, not more than 10 reps, on the 3rd day add exercise 3, 1 set, not more than 10 reps, on the 4th day add exercise 4, 1 set, not more than 10 reps, on the 5th day add exercise 5, set, not more than 10 reps. On the 6th day perform all exercises 1 set of not more than 5 reps. On the 10th day no more than 20 reps. On the 5th week increase reps, on the 7th week add 1 set of reps to each exercise, on the 8th week add (a set of reps to each exercise, on the 9th week add a set of reps to each excerise. Now you are performing 4 sets of reps in each exercise.

Increase the reps according to how strong your abdominals should be at this point in time. You can use this routine until you achieve the desired results.

SPOT SPECIALIZATION

1. exercise1
sit ups

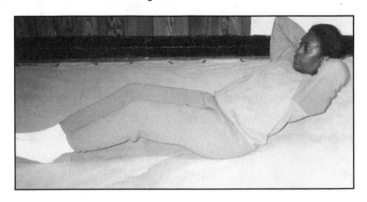

2. exercise2
standing twists

SPOT SPECIALIZATION

3. exercise3
twisting sit-ups

4. exercise 4
knee pushouts

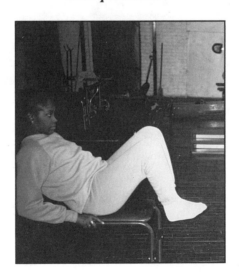

SPOT SPECIALIZATION

5. bend over twists

CHAPTER 19
WEIGHT-GAINING DRINKS AND FOODS

This chapter will cover tried and tested drinks and foods which have added pounds and pounds of healthy muscles on men and women over the years. Please read on.

The following instructions tell you what to put into your weight gaining drinks and how to make them from vegetarian sources. Consult your doctor and check that you are not contradicting his/her recommendations.

Drinks

Drink No. 1 Avocado Punch

To make 4 drinking glasses of avocado punch, peel one large ripe avocado, scoop out the pulp, place in blender, add 8 tablespoons of soya milk powder, and four tablespoons of any sweetener of your choice, then add 32 glasses of water, blend, pour into glass, sip slowly. Note: In all of the drink recipes given, you can use one glass of liquid soya milk, and 2 glasses of water instead.

Drink No. 2 Peanut Punch

To make 4 drinking glasses of peanut punch, place 8 heaped tablespoons of peanut butter in your blender, then add 8 heaped tablespoons of soya milk powder, sweetener of your choice, 32 glasses of water, blend, then pour into glass, sip slowly.

Drink No. 3 Banana Punch

To make 4 drinking glasses of banana punch, place 4 large ripe (spotted) bananas in your blender, then add 8 heaped tablespoons of soya milk powder, sweetener of your choice, 32 glasses of water, blend, pour into glass, sip slowly.

Drink No. 4 Papaya (Paw-Paw) Punch

To make 4 drinking glasses of papaya punch, peel one medium sized papaya (approximately 2 lbs.), remove the seeds, slice the pulp, place in blender, then add 8 heaped tablespoons of soya milk powder, 32 glasses of water, sweetener of your choice, blend, then pour into glass, sip slowly.

Drink No. 5 Mango Punch

To make 4 drinking glasses of mango punch, peel 2 large ripe mangos (approximately 3/4 lb.), slice them, removing the pulp, place in blender, then add 8 heaped tablespoons of soya milk powder, 3 glasses of water, sweetener of your choice, blend, then pour into glass, sip slowly.

Sweeteners

I personally recommend that you first taste the drink, without any sweetener. If you like the taste, drink it as is. You can add blackstrap molasses, brown sugar, soya condensed milk, corn syrup, etc.

Weight Gaining Foods

Recipe No. I

Stewed Potatoes, Rice & Salad

Stewed Potatoes:

1. Cut up one stem of scallion (chive), 1 small carrot, 1/2 of a small onion, 2 cloves of garlic, one stem parsley, 1 stem of celery 4" long with a few leaves, 1/2 of a small sweet pepper, 1/2 of a medium sized tomato. Heat the pot (stainless steel, iron or enamel-never use an aluminum pot), pour in about 5 tablespoons of corn oil or vegetable oil, then 3 tablespoons of soy sauce, heat for a while, then add all the ingredients, 1/2 cup of water, and cook for 2 minutes.

2. Add 1 pound of white potatoes, a tablespoonful of vegetarian margarine, 4 cups of water. Cover, stir every 5 minutes and once the contents of the pot begin to boil, test every ten minutes to see if potatoes are cooked. Let it simmer, and when the gravy is to your liking, turn off stove.

Rice:

To cook brown rice follow instructions on package, do not add salt, just water. Boil 2 cups rice.

Salad:

Slice one medium-sized cucumber, 1/2 small carrot, 1/2 small onion, 2 cloves of garlic, small sweet pepper, medium-sized tomato. Sprinkle one teaspoonful of apple cider vinegar on all ingredients, mixing them up with your hand or a spoon, then serve.

This recipe serves 3 adults or 2 adults and two small children.

Recipe No. 2

Vegetables, Rice & Salad.

1. Same as No.1 in recipe 1.

2. Add a large bundle of patchoi, cut into small pieces, cut 2 medium-sized carrots into strips, slice one small onion, slice 2 small turnip, slice stem broccoli, slice one medium tomato, slice one medium sweet pepper add ½ cup of water, one tablespoon of vegetarian margarine and cover. When pot begins to boil, check it every 5 minutes until pot simmers down. Turn off stove.

Rice:

Same as recipe 1.

Salad:

Same as recipe 1.

Recipe No. 3

Vegetable Vegetarian Soup

Two medium-sized carrots diced, slice one large sweet pepper, slice one medium beet root, add 1 lb. white potatoes, 1/2 lb yam (sweet potatoes), add one medium-sized tomato sliced, add water to cover all ingredients, add 1/2 onion sliced or chopped, 3 cloves garlic, 3 tablespoons of vegetarian margarine, celery (a piece about 5 inches long) chopped, stem of parsley, 1/2 small turnip chopped piece of broccoli 5 inches long chopped. Cover pot, let everything come to a boil, then add 2 tablespoons of soy sauce, test potatoes. When cooked, turn off the stove and after 5 minutes, serve.

Recipe No. 4

Stewed Red Beans, with Vegetable Pelau and Salad

1/2 lb red beans, oil, sugar, onion, 2 cloves garlic, 2 stems scallion (chive), stem celery, small carrot, half sweet pepper, ketchup, soy sauce and 1 tablespoon soya margarine.

1 Burst beans with garlic.

2. Slice onion, garlic, chive, celery, carrot, sweet pepper.

3. Put iron pot to heat, when hot, pour in two pot- spoons of oil. When oil is hot pour in 1/2 pot-spoon sugar, stir till golden brown, add onion, garlic, etc., then add 1/2 pot-spoon ketchup and 1/2 pot-spoon soy sauce. Stir up all ingredients then add soya margarine, stir and add red beans, then add 1/2 cup water, simmer down to taste.

Vegetable Pelau

3 medium carrots, 1 large sweet pepper, 1large onion , 3 long scallion stems, 2 large stems celery, oil, sugar,1/2 pot- spoon ketchup, 1/2 pot spoon soy sauce, 1/2 tablespoon soya margarine, 3 cups rice.

1. Put pot to heat, then add oil. When oil is hot pour in 1/2 pot-spoon sugar, stir till golden brown
2. Add vegetables, stir for 1 minute, then add the rest of the ingredients. Add 4 cups water, cook for 5 minutes.
3. Add 3 cups rice, cook on low heat till rice is cooked.

Salad:

1 Large cucumber, 1 large tomato, 1 sweet pepper, 3 large leaves lettuce

1. Wash and slice tomato, sweet pepper and cucumber (peel cucumber optional).
2. Wash lettuce leaves and cut up small.
3. Mix all ingredients together, throw some apple cider vinegar over salad (optional).

Serves 5 adults or 4 adults, 2 children.

Now you have five great health-weight building drinks and four great health-weight building recipes.

Please note: I personally do not use any kind of oils in my cooking, so you can use vegetable margarine in place of oil.

You can use soy sauce to brown your cook-up (pelau) instead of brown sugar.

CHAPTER 20

WEIGHT-REDUCING DRINKS AND FOODS

This chapter will cover tested and proven drinks and foods which will make you lose weight safely and healthy.

You must consult your doctor, show her the drinks and foods given here and ask her opinion. All the information given here is sound and health-building.

Drinks

Drink No. 1 Soya Punch

To make 4 glasses of soya punch pour 3 1/2 glasses of water in your blender, add 6 tablespoons of soya milk powder, 4 tablespoons of soya protein powder, blend. You can drink a glass of this nutritious high protein drink at 4 different intervals during the day. Or you can use soya drink.

Drink No. 2 Soya/Pineapple Punch

To make 4 glasses of soya/pineapple punch, peel one small pineapple, slice the pulp, put in blender, add 3 1/2 glasses of water, 6 tablespoons of soya milk, 4 tablespoons of soya protein powder, blend. You can drink a glass at 4 different intervals during the day. Shake or blend each time before drinking.

Drink No. 3 Soya-Papaya (Paw-Paw) Punch

To make 4 glasses of soya-papaya punch, peel one small papaya (3/4 lb.), slice pulp, put in blender, add 6 tablespoons of soya milk, 3 tablespoons of soya protein powder, 3½ glasses water, blend. You can drink a glass at different intervals during the day.

Drink No. 4 Citrus Drink

Squeeze 5 large grapefruits, 5 oranges, 10 tangerines, remove seeds, but not the pulp. Do not add water. Drink a glass at 4 different intervals during the day.

Reducing Foods

Recipe No. 1 Vegetable-Vegetarian Soup

Slice or dice 1 stem of scallion (chive), 1 stem of parsley, stem of celery, 2 onions, 3 cloves of garlic, 1 medium tomato, 1 medium carrot, medium beet root, 1 medium sweet pepper. Add 2 tablespoons of soy sauce, 2 tablespoons of vegetarian margarine, 3 medium-sized white potatoes. Add water to cover ingredients, test potatoes occasionally. When cooked, turn off stove 5 minutes later.

Recipe No. 2 Stewed Red Kidney Beans with Whole-wheat Bread and Salad

To make one serving of red kidney beans, cut dice or slice 1 small carrot, 1/2 turnip, 5 inches of celery, stem of parsley, 1/2 small onion, 2 cloves, 2 garlic, 1 stem of scallion (chive). Stir them up, heat your pot or saucepan, pouring in 4 tablespoons of soya, corn, or vegetable oil. When hot, put in all the above ingredients, then add 2 tablespoons of soy sauce, stir, add 1 cup water. Place 6 ounces red kidney beans in pot add water until all ingredients are covered. After boiling for ten minutes, test beans, when beans are cooked turn off stove 5 minutes after. To avoid burning the beans, you can add hot water as necessary when cooking.

When cool, you can eat the beans with 3 slices of whole-wheat bread, and a salad as follows.

Salad

Slice 1 medium tomato, 1 small cucumber, 1 small carrot (or you can grate it), 1 small sweet pepper, 1/2 small onion. 2 cloves garlic, 2 leaves lettuce.

Recipe No. 3 Steamed Vegetables and Salad

Salad as in recipe no. 2, plus steamed cabbage, steamed carrots, 2 boiled white potatoes with 2 tablespoons of vegetarian margarine.

Recipe No. 4 Corn Soup

Boil 2 corns with medium sweet pepper sliced or chopped, 1 medium tomato, 1 small carrot, 1/2 small onion, 2 cloves garlic, 5 inches celery, 1 stem parsley, 2 tablespoons of soy sauce. Add water to cover all ingredients, add 2 tablespoons of vegetarian margarine. Let all ingredients boil, test corn, when cooked let boil for 3 more minutes, cool then eat corn and drink soup.

To lose weight you should eat low calorie nutritious meals and consume nutritious drinks, so you can use a combination of food once daily and 3 or 4 glasses of any of the drinks for the rest of the day along with supplements.

CHAPTER 21

FIGHTING COLDS, GALLSTONES, KIDNEY STONES, POLIO, HEMORRHOIDS, HEADACHES, PIMPLES

Colds, gall stones, kidney stones etc., are the products of a faulty diet most of the time. Therefore to correct these problems is not as simple as taking this drug or that drug to correct it, as it will appear again and again, and you might also have to deal with the side effects of the drugs.

Please note: This is not meant to contradict any treatment you may be undergoing from your doctor or physician. By all means obey your doctor.

I have myself suffered multiple physical ailments, from migraine headaches, hernia, kidney stones etc. Through proper dieting, I have been able to defeat all of these ailments. Not only have I been able to solve my own problems, but I have also helped scores of people correct their own physical ailments.

You are advised to consult your physician or doctor before embarking on any plans given here.

Fighting Colds

Colds can be prevented, or the term of the cold cut short by megavitamin therapy. I personally took up to 22,000 mg of vitamin C to combat a cold which came on me for some reason or the other after I had not taken any vitamin C supplements for several days.

I personally take 4,000 to 6,000 mg of vitamin C daily in the summer and increase this to 8,000 to 10,000 mg daily in the winter. I also use Zinc supplements, which fight infections, plus a vitamin/ mineral tablet along with a B complex 50 tablet.

Gall Stones and Kidney Stones

These stones can be successfully expelled from the body by using herbal treatment. Several years ago, I suffered with kidney stones: my feet were swollen, I had trouble urinating, it was very painful. I began using parsley tea, drinking 2 to 4 glasses each day. The swelling left my feet and I began urinating

freely. From time to time I still drink a few glasses of parsley tea, as it is good.

To make 4 glasses of parsley tea, pour 4 glasses of water in a stainless steel enamel or iron pot, but <u>never use an aluminum pot.</u> Let water begin to boil, then wash 5 stems of parsley, put them in the pot, cover it, turn off the stove, let parsley tea cool. Do not add any sweetener, use just as it is naturally. Note: Women near, during or just after their menstrual period, and pregnant women should not use parsley tea.

Polio

Nutritional scientists and doctors who are nutritionally inclined, have had amazing results with megavitamin theraphy in preventing and stopping polio.

Hemorrhoids (piles)

In the past, and again recently, I have used vitamin E and vitamin B6 to treat hemorrhoids with success. Over ten years ago a friend was operated on for hemorrhoids and it returned. He then came to me, and I told him what to do, and wrote down on a piece of paper what he should purchase. I have seen him many times since then, and as a result of following my guidelines, there has been no further problem.

The remedy for hemorrhoids is eating good healthy vegetarian foods. Direct treatment is one 100 IU vitamin E capsule to be taken after your last meal at night, along with a vitamin/mineral tablet, B complex 50 tablet, and one vitamin B6 tablet 20-25 mg. Twice daily, wash your rear, then pierce one 100 IU vitamin E capsule, pasting the vitamin E liquid on the affected area (this is to be done after rising in the mornings and last thing at night). If you follow this you should have positive relief in 7 to 10 days.

Migraine Headaches

I personally make it a duty never to take any kind of drugs, whether it be aspirin or cocaine. You can't take a painkiller as it would do just that-kill the pain, <u>not the cause of the pain</u>. Proper nutrition goes to the cause, so you get a cure.

I have treated not only myself for migraine headaches in the past, but many other persons using proper diet and megavitamin therapy. I usually tell migraine sufferers gradually to eliminate all animal products from their diet, also chocolate, coffee, tea etc. In all cases, the migraine headaches went.

Besides the vegetarian diet, the following health food supplements were

used: vegetarian vitamin and mineral tablet, 2,000 mg vitamin C, B complex "50" tablets, 2 teaspoons apple cider vinegar in one glass of water morning and night.

Pimples

People with pimples can usually get rid of them by eliminating milk and milk products from their diets, adding vitamin/mineral tablet, 2,000 mg vitamin C, B complex "50" tablet, 2 brewer's yeast tablets daily. If this fails to clear up the problem, change gradually to a vegetarian diet.

These are not meant to change what your doctor may prescribe, but if you show your doctor this book, you will probably find that she encourages you to follow my recommendations. Remember, there are hundreds of doctors who not only share my belief in nutritional therapy, but are using this type of therapy daily to cure myriads of ailments.

CHAPTER 22

VEGETARIANISM

When I use the term 'vegetarianism', I speak of a real vegetarian, a vegan, one who does not consume any animal products whatsoever. I have been a vegetarian for over eighteen years now and have no regrets. I no longer suffer from migraine headaches, kidney stones, colds, etc.

I remember my first serious encounter with vegetarianism. I was suffering with a pain in my left knee, and I went to the doctor, who gave me 120 pain-killing tablets, advising me how many to take each day, and asking me to return to him when they were finished. At that time I was reading a book on nutrition by a female author, who said that her personal research led her to believe that the poisonous toxins from animal flesh, when consumed, tend to settle in the joints of the body, e.g. knees, elbows, ankles, wrists, etc., which might be weak or have a minor injury. These poisons accumulate to a point where they begin to cause pain. The cure: stop eating those products. I did not use the pain killers and I became a vegetarian.

I began eating meat again, and the migraine headaches, kidney stones etc. returned. This time I stopped eating animal flesh and never turned back. The first thing I noticed was that I had more energy, I stopped feeling tired and pooped out at nights, I had more endurance, and I enjoyed better health.

I will deal here with common fallacies about total vegetarianism (veganism):

1.   Vegetarian protein is not complete. This is so far from the truth that it is ridiculous. The first thing you must observe is that all the best sources of animal protein are themselves vegetarian: the cow, goat, sheep, etc. These animals have intestines similar to humans. Carnivorous animals have shorter intestines.

Two pounds of soy flour contain as much protein as six dozen eggs or fifteen quarts of milk.

The proteins of legumes and leafy vegetables supplement remarkably well with those of cereals, and have been determined to be as efficient as proteins of animal origin.

2.   Every single, isolated nutrient necessary for the survival and well-being of mankind can be found in the vegetable kingdom. Split peas, lentils, or other legumes, nuts, common greens and olives prepared in a variety of

ways help take the place of milk and eggs, both from the standpoint of enjoyment and nutritional advantages

3. The very structure of the human teeth shows us without doubt that mankind was originally created to eat vegetarian foods. Take for example the sheep, goat, cow and other vegetarian animals. Compare their teeth structure with the wolf, dog, lion, tiger etc., all carnivorous animals. I think you will see the point I am making.

4. There are even some people who live exclusively on a fruit diet and are healthy (fruitarians).

5. The recipes and drinks recommended in this book contain all the nutrients necessary for a good healthy, vigorous body. The soya bean and soya products are vastly superior in quality, protein and other nutrients than any animal product. Besides the quality of meat and meat products leave a lot to be desired.

The cruelty meted out to animals just to increase their size quickly, or to produce more milk, should leave you thinking. The hormones and other injections given to them to produce growth must also be considered. Take a look at the poultry industry. I have seen and heard first hand what goes on in poultry-rearing. I saw dead chickens, trampled by other chickens, and their flesh looked blue. The man in charge of rearing them told me that it was unsafe to eat them before a certain time period, which allowed the drugs to leave their system. Then the color of the flesh returned to normal. But what guarantees do we have?

Remember, too, all the warnings about "Salmonella" in eggs. Must we take these chances with our well-being when there is a safe alternative? Even the seas, lakes and rivers, which at one point in time were considered good sources of healthy food, are risky. Fish now are very hazardous to eat, contaminated somewhere along the line by pesticides, industrial chemicals, parasites, natural toxins, toxic metals, micro-organisms, etc.

Damage to the human system from eating contaminated fish ranges from cancer, damage to the human nerve cells, kidney damage, hearing problems, damage to your mental development, visual problems, etc.

6. Many writers on nutrition insist that vegans (total vegetarians) must

get their vitamin B12 from animal sources. Nothing could be further from the truth, as this vitamin is easily available from vegetarian sources such as brewer's yeast wheat germ, etc., and as a vitamin B12 supplement from vegetable sources.

7.   When you are a vegetarian, your body does not have to cope with the poisons left in the system from animal products, so naturally you feel better, look better and enjoy life more. Many doctors are now beginning to criticize milk. It is well known by dietitians that milk is not essential to health.

8.   Some body-builders have turned to vegetarianism but still use dairy products or eggs. But you can gain healthy muscular body weight without consuming any animal product whatsoever. Read over the sections dealing with diet, etc.

To those of you who are religious, remember that before the flood (in Prophet Noah's time p.b.u.h) the whole world was vegetarian.. The Almighty Creator in his wisdom permitted mankind after the flood to partake of the clean animals for food, as all vegetation was destroyed outside the Ark. If man lived for hundreds of years before the flood, in a healthy state on a vegetarian diet isn't that possible today? Think about it.

People change to a vegetarian diet for many reasons. Some are:
1.   For health reasons
2.   Personal preference
3.   Because of the cruelty meted out to animals for meat, milk production
4.   For a change
5.   For other reasons.

References
1.   The Animal Connection (Cancer and Other Diseases from Animals and Foods of Animal Origin) by Agatha M. Thrash, MD. and Calvin L. Thrash, Jr., MD. (New Lifestyle Books, Seale AL 36875), p. 4

2.   The Animal Connection by Agatha M. Thrash, MD. and Calvin L. Thrash, Jr., MD., p. 42

3.   The Animal Connection by Agatha M. Thrash, MD. and Calvin L.

Thrash, Jr., MD., p. 43.

CHAPTER 23

HERBS

I will deal briefly with herbs here, as I point out the benefits of using herbs. Herbs are essential for your well-being as they contain vitamins, minerals and other properties.

I would list just a few, stating briefly some of their benefits:

Parsley:

I have mentioned in Chapter 21 some of the benefits of parsley. Tea made of parsley leaves has an old reputation as one of the best diuretic remedies. It was used by early healers as a panacea for kidney ailments and in the treatment of stones and urinary complaints. It is also recommended for jaundice.

Sorrel:

This is used as a beverage and as medicine. In the Caribbean, this is drunk in great quantities as a beverage, especially at the end of the year when it is plentiful and cheap.

Ginger:

This is used as a beverage and as medicine in the Caribbean. This is drunk in great quantities as a beverage, and I personally am fond of it . As a medicine it is good to use as a gargle for sore throat, it's a good remedy for the cold, indigestion, heartburn, and poor circulation. It makes a good tea, and generates a warm feeling in your body.

Anise (Pimpinella Snisum):

Aniseed tea is prepared by pouring boiling water on the seeds; then it is used for catarrhs and colds. It is especially liked by infants, it helps in dry coughs and in asthmatic attacks, it is reputed to be an immediate palliative.[2]

Devil's Claw; Harpagophytum Procumbens:

Very effective in arthritis, rheumatism and gout.[3]

Thyme (Thymus Serpyllum):

Tea made of thyme can be used after meals as a digestive help, but its fame is mostly connected with its properties as a calming agent on the mucous tissues and as a dissolver of phlegm. It is also advised for flatulence.[4]

Golden Seal Root: Hydrastis Canadensis:

Affections of the liver, especially cancer in the early stage which is marked by poor appetite and digestion, constipation etc.

Vervain Blue (Verbena Off icinalis):

Old doctors prescribed it for wounds, stones, headaches, malaria, piles, childbirth, and so on.

Nowadays, it is employed as a nerve-calming beverage and it is helpful against the discomfort of colds.[6]

REFERENCES

1. <u>Herbal Tea Book</u> by Ann Adrian and Judith Dennis (Royal Inc., p.2)
2. <u>Herbal Tea Book</u> by Ann Adrian and Judith Dennis, p. 2.
3. <u>The Metu Neter Herbal Guide</u> by Ra Un Nefer Amenl (Khamit Corp. P.0. Box 28 Bronx, NY 0462), p. 3.
4. <u>Herbal Tea Book</u> by Ann Adrian and Judith Dennis, p. 28.
5. <u>The Metu Neter Herbal Guide</u> by Ra Un Nefer Amen, p. 4.
6. <u>Herbal Tea Book</u> by Ann Adrian and Judith Dennis, p. 29.

CHAPTER 24

SMOKING

One of the greatest evils to befall mankind is the disgusting habit of smoking, whether it be cigars, cigarettes, pipes, tobacco, marijuana, cocaine, etc.

I, personally cannot stand the smell of cigarette, cigar or marijuana smoke. It stifles me, it gives me a headache. Smoking causes lung cancer and other damage. Smoking one cigarette destroys 25 mg or more of vitamin C in the body, which is needed greatly as the human body does not manufacture or store vitamin C. Smoking is one of the causes of bad breath, staining of the teeth, fingernails, etc.

Smoking is an international nuisance, affecting not only smokers, but non-smokers as well.

Smoking is addiction at it's worst. Cigarettes are easily available, destructive, and sells faster than some foods. Mankind has truly taken leave of its senses and thrown caution to the wind.

I say put a total ban on cigarette smoking in all public vehicles, buses, trains, taxis, planes, stores, supermarkets, on the road etc. The message must be strong: if you must smoke then smoke at home.

Cigarette smoking causes lung cancer, heart disease etc. It does further damage to persons suffering from diabetes, hypertension, stomach ulcers, etc.

An article in the Post, states that a medical researcher, Dr. Wolfgang Vogel says, marijuana apparently is likely to produce cancer as cigarette tobacco because pot-smokers usually hold the smoke in their lungs as long as possible. [1]

Smoking marijuana damages the brain and other parts of the body.

Cigarette smokers who drop their cigarettes from their lips instead of holding them in their fingers run a far higher risk of developing chronic bronchitis, according to a report in the British Medical Journal. [2]

Smoking cocaine does untold damage to the brain, body, etc. It dominates the users and changes them literally to Zombies.

There is strong evidence that pregnant women who smoke cigarettes are increasing the risk of death of their babies

What more evidence would any sensible human being want, to persuade them to stop smoking?

REFERENCES

1. <u>Mega-vitamin Therapy</u> by Ruth Adams and Frank Murray (Larchmont Books, 390 Fifth Avenue New York, N.Y. 10017, p. 244.

2. <u>Mega-vitamin Therapy</u> by Ruth Adams and Frank Murray, p. 243.

3. <u>Mega-vitamin Therapy</u> by Ruth Adams and Frank Murray. D. 241.

CHAPTER 25

ALCOHOL

Another evil to befall mankind is the consumption of alcohol, which is so evil that it not only damages the health of the users, but also kills the users and in that process sometimes kills those who do not use it.

The Holy Quran makes it abundantly clear in Sura 5 verses 90 and 91.

90. One who believes <u>Intoxicants</u> and gambling, (Dedication of) Stones, And (divination by) arrows are an abomination, - <u>of Satan's handiwork: eschew such (abomination!, that ye may prosper.</u>

91. <u>Satan's plan is (but to excite enmity and hatred between you, with intoxicants and gambling and hinder you from the remembrance of Allah, and from prayer: will ye not then abstain?</u>

Let us deal first with the damage and violence alcohol causes to be directed to those who do not even use it Then we will deal with the physical. moral and spiritual damage done to the individual.

You may have read headlines or sub headlines like these, with an accompanying story:

Drunken driver crashes into vehicle 3 killed 4 hospitalized
Drunken man runs amok, 2 killed 5 seriously injured
Drunken husband beats wife to death
Drunken father seriously injures child (or children)
Drunken worker fired after repeated warnings
Drunken man dies in fire accidentally caused
Drunken father rapes daughter

Just recently a drunken woman was killed after coming home from a party. She slipped between the carriages of the train onto the tracks, and was crushed to death. I could go on and on.

Now let us deal with the physical damage done to the individual. Alcoholism is one of the most damaging health problems facing the world today, especially

Western countries and non Islamic countries. Alcohol damages the brain, liver, stomach, heart and other organs. It often leads to malnutrition as it destroys essential nutrients. Alcohol drinkers frequently fail to eat properly.

It causes the user to feel confused, tense, etc. The damage is done spiritually also as the person no longer wants to pray, or even thinks that praying is in vain. He or she loses faith in the Almighty Creator. One of the Hadith of the Prophet Muhammad (p.b.u.h) says there is a curse on those who make intoxicants, those who buy it to sell, those who serve it, and those who use it

Every word of that is true, as the only sure way of avoiding being an alcoholic is to avoid all intoxicants totally. If you never drink you can never become an alcoholic.

You may say that many persons drink intoxicants casually and are not alcoholics as yet. Only time will tell - Alcoholics can come from those who consume alcohol casually or regularly not from those who never use intoxicants

All who drink socially, even if they are quite moderate drinkers could be prone to the disease of alcoholism, the NCA points out.

Alcohol is one of the greatest known causes of both using up and washing the B vitamins out of the body.

Alcohol is a factor in at least half the motor vehicle fatalities each year.

REFERENCES

1.   <u>Mega- vitamin Therapy</u> by Ruth Adams and Frank Murray (Larchmont Books, 390 fifth Avenue, New York, N. Y. 10017) p.32

2.   <u>Know Your Nutrition,</u> by Linda Clark (Keats publishing, Inc., *Box* 876, 36 Crove Street, New Canaan, Connecticut 06840) p.74

3.   <u>Mega Vitamin Therapy</u> by Ruth Adams and Frank Murray, p.17

CHAPTER 26

HOW TO TAKE CONTROL OF YOUR MIND

The easiest way to control a person is to control his or her mind. I always teach my children and grandchildren that what goes into your head by your eyes comes out of your mouth. I have known persons who can hardly carry on an intelligent conversation, for the simple reason that they never spend time educating themselves. I do not mean actually going to a university or college, although that is desirable; what I mean is that some persons go through the same unproductive stagnant cycle each day, each week, each month, each year and wonder why they are not progressing. They might earn a better salary than the other guy, but he seems to be making far more progress, he is more knowledgeable, people always seem to want to associate with him and ask his opinion, etc.

If you read only trash, if you only listen to stupid conversations and idle talk, if you waste your time doing nothing, what do you expect to be able to say? How do you expect to measure up to one who is well read, who weighs matters, who investigates, who researches, who practices what he learns constructively?

I make it my business not to indulge in reading or viewing pornography. I do not use obscene words, as that is the lowest form of verbal expression. I make it a duty to purchase educational books. I look at meaningful programs on TV, and I listen to meaningful programs on the radio. I try to associate as much as possible with persons with intelligent aspirations, and over the years the Almighty Creator (Allah) has blessed me with knowledge in history, Afrikan and general, martial arts, health, psychology, food production, business, religion, art, physical fitness, etc.

I have worked as a labourer, draughts man, mechanical engineering, builder (house construction), physical fitness instructor, martial arts instructor, hardware dealer, transport (driving own van and truck), installation of cable TV food vendor, author (on several subjects), etc.

What I have seen without doubt is that whatever you like to do, regardless of how hard it is you get it done, and whatever you don't like to do, even if it

is easy, it becomes hard to do. The reason for that is that, 'It's all in the mind.'

Now I return to the subject of this chapter: <u>How to take control</u> <u>of your</u> <u>mind</u>.

This can be done in 12 easy steps

1. Make sure you want something good, which will be your goal. Any honorable profession would be an example.

2. Keep this in your mind.

3. Talk to as many successful persons in that profession as you can

4. Even though you might not have the money at the moment to pursue that profession academically keep it in your mind, and devise plans to raise the money to pursue that profession

5. Avoid persons who would discourage you.

6. Believe in yourself, believe "you can do it and act decisively on it. This very book took me over 30 years in research, and ten years to prepare this final format after planning, sifting and making sure that what reached my readers were practical ideas.

7. Never follow the crowd, you must always decide for yourself after weighing all the facts carefully .

8. Write down your goal on a piece of paper, say how you intend to achieve this goal and read it aloud, after your prayer to the Almighty Creator on mornings and after you pray at nights. Repeat it to yourself several times each day. You must never give up, never procrastinate (putting off - postponing).

9. Let's be specific. You decide to be a salesman but the particular field of sales which you want to pursue is costly, you then look to another field of sales which takes little or no investment and avoids that (temporary) diversion to achieve your main or your life's goal.

10. The key word is persistence I have seen examples of this, in my own life. I started to build a house when I was a young man, a certain old man passed by. He told me, "The way you are going, you will die before you

live in that house" He angered me so much that I silently vowed to prove him wrong, as I knew that everyday would draw me closer to the completion of that house. I proved him so wrong, that not only did I live to occupy the house, but also my children and my grandchildren, at that same house I have given free rooms to many persons who were in need. This shows that once you have a goal and you really work hard towards that goal, you will succeed. To build this house I started as a salesman, my first week's commission from those sales was $4.00, and when the man paid me, he said, 'How much money did you have last week' I replied none, he said, 'well, this week you have $4.00." The next week, my commission amounted to $10.00 and he didn't have to tell me anything. I knew what I wanted and I never stopped I continued, I was persistent.

12. In this instance, your goal is good health and you should decide now, after sifting all that you have read, that you want to be healthy, not just to exist anyhow, but to be 'healthy', so decide that all your actions must contribute to bringing about this state of being healthy. You must be persistent, even if you falter sometimes. Keep your eyes on the final goal and you will achieve it.

CHAPTER 27

FINAL ANALYSIS

You have just about finished reading this book, but you can put it down and forget what you have just read.

No amount of knowledge can benefit anyone unless you put it into practical use regularly.

Examples

1. You have a beautiful car, but you shine it, check it out, and take so much care, that you hardly want to use it, as you are afraid that you might get it scratched or dented. Instead, you take the train or the bus, but in the first place, you bought the car to escape from these pressures (hustling for the bus or the train). So the car actually begins to be a burden.

2. On occasions, I have recommended certain foods, supplements, drinks, etc., to particular people. Then they tell me that these things aren't working, but when I questioned them, it turned out that they did buy what I recommended but they hardly used them, so the benefits? Benefits were minimal.

3. I've made recommendations to certain people, but they've never acted on them. Therefore they got no results, they just kept on procrastinating .

4. Then there are those who acted on the information and got exceptionally good results. So the final decision rests with you, as only "you can make it work for yourself." Don't go through life wishing. Wishing in itself is good, but it must be backed up by action. Give it a try and see how your health improves. You have to live in your body every day until you die, so you can know when you feel sick, and when you are improving. You be the judge.

5 . Just recently when I went to Jumah, Muslim's Friday prayer and Kutbah (sermon), the Imam said there was once a pious Muslim, who when asked, whom he copied or which pious person inspired him to be so. He answered none. He said that when he looked around and saw ignorance and unrighteousness, he said to himself how ugly all this looked and he strove by the help of Allah to avoid all this ignorance and unrighteousness .

6. The path to success, whether it be business, sport, home life, public life, achievements academically or otherwise, righteousness etc., is to investigate and when you are convinced that this is the path to success in whatever field, seek Allah's guidance (in the first place and the last) and do not waiver. And even if you stumble, you have not fallen, if you fall, you get back up, so never give up, be persistent.

7 . This book deals with nutrition and in short <u>good health,</u> to attain good health you have to be vigilant, I never consume any packaged goods, if I have not read the label first. When you read, <u>it may</u> <u>contain animal or vegetable fat.</u> Which animal?

　　　Even persons who use meat should be careful, as that animal fat might just be <u>pork fat</u>.

　　　You must not look for the easy way out always (be vigilant). Be careful about what you eat, what you drink what you think.

I always tell my children, you can only speak what is in your head, and if you have rubbish in your head, then you will speak rubbish. If you have good knowledge in your head, then your speech will make sense. I always remind my children that 'you are what you eat'. You can be healthy, if you eat health-building foods, if you consume health-building drinks, and if you think clean.

　　　This book contains the key to good health, you can use this key to open the door to good health or you can refuse to use the key and drag through life.

ACKNOWLEDGMENTS

First I must thank Almighty Allah for the knowledge he has given to me, and kept me up, even sometimes when I was discouraged.

I must thank my daughter Nilaja Mandisa Tayo, who wasn't even born when I first began to do research for this book. She so patiently typed the manuscript for me, correcting errors which were mostly due to my <u>mind</u> being ahead of <u>my pen.</u>

I thank my mother, who persistently sought to educate me at all costs although she was poor.

I thank my father who never completed his elementary education, but had an insatiable thirst for reading.

I thank my grandfather (maternal) who I never knew, but for what I heard he was a just man, if he had lived longer, my life would have been easier.

I thank my daughters, Ayodele and Alafia, for posing for the exercise photos. I thank Carl Greenidge, my bodybuilding student, for posing for the exercise photos. I thank my stepfather (deceased) who in his own way contributed to my education. I thank all who I forgot to thank and last but not the least, Sekou Tafari, my publisher who saw the value in publishing this work, I have known him for over thirty years.

I thank the following publishers and authors for the permission they have granted to me, to make use of references and quotations from their publications:

Know Your Nutrition, by Linda Clark (Keats Publishing Inc.) Mega-Vitamin Therapy by Ruth Adams and Frank Murray (Larchmont Books) Herbal Tea Book by Ann Adams and Judith Dennis (Royal Publication Inc.)

I am also thankful for the information quoted briefly from:
<u>The Animal Connection</u> by Agatha M. Thrash, M.D. and Calvin Thrash, Jr., M.D. (New Lifestyle Books)
<u>The Metu Neter Herbal Guide</u> by Ra Un Nefer (Amen Khamit Corp.)

NOTES

NOTES

ALSO DISTRIBUTED BY

FRONTLINE DISTRIBUTION INTERNATIONAL, INC.

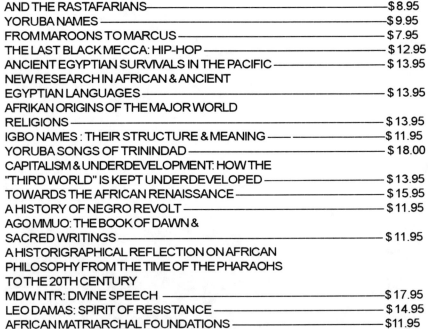

RASTAFARI, A WAY OF LIFE ———————————————————$ 16.95
RASTARIAN VIEW OF MARCUS MOSIAH GARVEY ——————$ 14.95
AFRICA: ROOTS OF JAMAICAN CULTURE ——————————$ 14.95
THE GROUNDING WITH MY BROTHERS ———————————$ 9.95
PAN-AFRICANISM AND ZIONISM ———————————————$ 16.95
THE RASTAFARI IBLE —————————————————————$ 12.95
THE WORLD'S SIXTEEN CRUCIFIED SAVIORS ————————$ 17.95
THE AFRICA CENTERED PERSPECTIVE OF HISTORY———— $ 13.95
BLACK SISTERS, SPEAKOUT —————————————————$ 13.95
EUROPEAN COLONIAL DESPOTISM ——————————————$ 20.00
AFRICAN SYSTEMS OF SCIENCE TECHNOLOGY
AND ART ——————————————————————————————$ 14.95
READINGS IN PRECOLONIAL CENTRAL AFRICA———————$ 13.95
INTRODUCTION TO THE STUDY OF AFRICAN
CLASSICAL CIVILIZATIONS ————————————————————$ 15.00
EMPEROR HAILE SELASSIE
AND THE RASTAFARIANS———————————————————————$ 8.95
YORUBA NAMES ————————————————————————————$ 9.95
FROM MAROONS TO MARCUS ——————————————————$ 7.95
THE LAST BLACK MECCA: HIP-HOP ————————————————$ 12.95
ANCIENT EGYPTIAN SURVIVALS IN THE PACIFIC —————— $ 13.95
NEW RESEARCH IN AFRICAN & ANCIENT
EGYPTIAN LANGUAGES —————————————————————— $ 13.95
AFRIKAN ORIGINS OF THE MAJOR WORLD
RELIGIONS ————————————————————————————— $ 13.95
IGBO NAMES : THEIR STRUCTURE & MEANING ——— ———$ 11.95
YORUBA SONGS OF TRININDAD ————————————————— $ 18.00
CAPITALISM & UNDERDEVELOPMENT: HOW THE
"THIRD WORLD" IS KEPT UNDERDEVELOPED ——————— $ 13.95
TOWARDS THE AFRICAN RENAISSANCE ———————————— $ 15.95
A HISTORY OF NEGRO REVOLT ————————————————— $ 11.95
AGO MMUO: THE BOOK OF DAWN &
SACRED WRITINGS ——————————————————————————— $ 11.95
A HISTORIGRAPHICAL REFLECTION ON AFRICAN
PHILOSOPHY FROM THE TIME OF THE PHARAOHS
TO THE 20TH CENTURY
MDW NTR: DIVINE SPEECH ———————————————————$ 17.95
LEO DAMAS: SPIRIT OF RESISTANCE ——————————————$ 14.95
AFRICAN MATRIARCHAL FOUNDATIONS ————————————$ 11.95
A-Z AFRICAN PROVERBS ————————————————————————$ 11.95
CULTURAL UNITY OF BLACK AFRICA———————————————$ 14.95
FOUNDATIONS OF AFRICAN THOUGHT —————————————$ 14.95
AFRICAN BACKGROUND TO
MEDICAL SCIENCE ————————————————————————————$ 15.95

ALSO DISTRIBUTED BY

FRONTLINE DISTRIBUTION INTERNATIONAL, INC.

PARISANS AND PROVINCIALS ——————— ————————$ 10.95
THE STATE AND ECONOMY OF
EARLY 20TH CENTURY ETHIOPIA————————————$ 15.95
PRE-COLONIAL CENTRAL AFRICA ————————————$ 13.95
ON THE WALLS OF MY BEING ——————————————$ 11.95
THE WORLD OF AFRICAN MUSIC ——————————————$ 20.00
MALE DAUGHTERS, FEMALE HUSBANDS ——————— $ 15.00
DELINKING ——————————————————————— $ 13.95
SAMORA MACHEL : A BIOGRAPHY ———————————— $ 15.00
THE DIFFICULT DIALOGUE ———————————————— $ 13.95
BOUNDS OF POSSIBILTY:
LEGACY OF STEVE BIKO ——————— ——————————$ 17.50
STAYING POWER ————————————————————— $ 19.95
SUGAR AND MODERN SLAVERY ——————————————— $ 17.50
WOMEN AND LABOR IN
TRINIDAD AND TOBAGO ———————————————————— $ 16.95
THE HEALERS ———————————————————————— $ 17.95
2,000 SEASONS ———————————————————————— $ 16.95
WOMEN AND THE ENVIRONMENT ——————————————— $ 15.95
ETHIOPIA UNDER MUSSOLINI —————————————————— $ 15.00
WOMEN AND HEALTH ——————————————————————— $ 15.95
AFRICAN WOMEN AND DEVELOPMENT ————————————— $ 15.00
COLOR, CLASS AND COUNTRY; EXPERIENCES
OF GENDER———————————————————————— $ 16.95
KWAME NKRUMAH: THE CONAKRY YEARS ———————————— $ 20.00
CLASS STRUGGLE IN AFRICA——————————————————— $ 3.95
NEO-COLONIALISM: THE LAST STATE
OF IMPERIALISM———————————— —————————— $ 15.00
TOWARDS COLONIAL FREEDOM——————————————————— $ 3.95
FORWARD EVER——————————————— ——————————$ 3.95
SOME ESSENTIAL FEATURES OF
NKRUMAISM———————————————————————————— $ 5.95
EDUARDO MONDLANE ————————————————————————— $ 7.95
SEKOU TOURE ————————————————————————————— $ 8.95
AFRICA ON THE MOVE —————————————————————— —$ 15.00
ISRAEL: AN APARTHEID STATE ——————————————————— $ 15.00
BLACK PEOPLE IN THE BRITISH EMPIRE:
AN INTRODUCTION——————————————————————— —$ 12.95
HUMAN DEVELOPMENT FROM AN AFRICAN
ANCESTRY ———————————————————————————— $ 16.95
DAUGHTER'S GRACE —————————————————————————— $ 11.95
RHYTHMS OF LIFE ——————————————————————— —$ 11.95
FROM OKPONKU ABU / POETRY——————————————————— $ 9.95

ALSO DISTRIBUTED BY

FRONTLINE DISTRIBUTION INTERNATIONAL, INC.

FORTUNE OF BEING YOURSELF ———————————————————————— $9.95
RADIANT WOMEN OF COLOR ——————————————————————— —$9.95
HOUSE OF BONDAGE ——————————————————————————$10.50
WORDS & MEANINGS OF THE YORUBA
LANGUAGE ——————————————————————————————$14.95

THE STRUGGLE CONTINUES ——————————————————————— $5.95
VOICE FROM CONAKRY ————————————————————————$5.95
CHALLENGE OF THE CONGO ————————————————————— $11.50

CHILDREN'S BOOKS

CHILDREN OF A HUNTER ————————————————————————$6.95
THE BRAVE PRINCESS SHANI ———————————————————— –$6.95
IN SEARCH OF A RASTAMAN ——————————————————— $6.95
THE CUNNING PRINCE AND THE WISE FOX————————————— $4.95
KONA: STORIES OF LOVE ——————————————————————–$7.95
STORM CHILD——————————————————————————— $7.95